MINECRAFT MASTER BUILDER

MINIGAMES

Published in 2022 by Mortimer Children's Books,
An Imprint of Welbeck Children's Limited,
part of Welbeck Publishing Group.
Based in London and Sydney.

Models built by: Ben Westwood

Designed, written and packaged by: Dynamo Limited
Design Manager: Sam James
Editorial Manager: Joff Brown
Production: Melanie Robertson

ISBN: 978 1 83935 152 5

Printed in Dongguan, China

10 9 8 7 6 5 4 3 2

All game information correct as of September 2021

MINECRAFT MASTER BUILDER
MINIGAMES

MORTIMER

CONTENTS

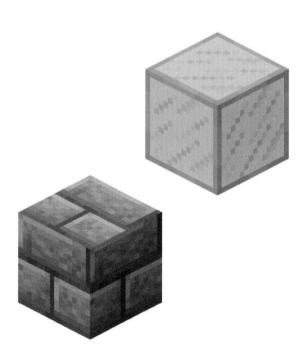

WELCOME TO MINECRAFT MINIGAMES!

So, you're a mega Minecraft fan and love building, exploring, and having adventures? Great, because you're in the right place to take your play to the next level and dive into the awesome world of Minecraft minigames! Time to set aside thoughts of the Overworld, the Nether, and the End to one side and tackle an exciting new experience...

WHAT IS A MINIGAME?

Minigames are fun builds where you can interact and compete against your Minecraft buddies. From quick games like obstacle and parkour courses to seriously speedy races or more complex quests that need survival skills, there are stacks of game types to test and tease you. Many minigames already exist and can be accessed through servers or subscription deals. That's all good, but the real fun is in creating your very own minigames!

GET REAL

Using your imagination, your building skills and your creative powers, you will soon be playing inside your own games. Can you imagine getting to participate in cool and crazy online battles and competitions in a world that you brought to life? Plus, your gaming friends will be there with you. Thanks to this epic step-by-step book, which has easy, intermediate, and master build levels, your visions will soon become reality!

PLAYING TOGETHER

NEW TO MINECRAFT?

If you're still new to the wonders of Minecraft, then don't sweat it. Just have fun and explore the game's basics in your own time, increasing your knowledge of building and progressing on the platform. Whether you play on PC, console, or mobile device, the action is pretty much limitless!

MULTIPLAYER CHOICES

Minecraft can be set up in either single player or multiplayer mode. Single player is great for beginners, especially in Easy or Peaceful mode, where someone new to the joys of Steve and Alex can soon come to grips with the landscape and challenges. Multiplayer is what you'll be itching to join, though, because this is where you and your friends can get together and play in your own Minecraft world.

STAYING SAFE ONLINE

Minecraft is one of the most popular games on the planet because it combines amazing building with fun. However, the most important part of the game is to stay safe when you are online.

Below are our tips for keeping safe:

- Tell a trusted adult what you're doing and ask before downloading anything
- Speak to a trusted adult if you are worried about anything
- Turn off chat
- Find a child-friendly server
- Only screenshare with real-life friends
- Watch out for viruses and malware
- Set a game-play time limit

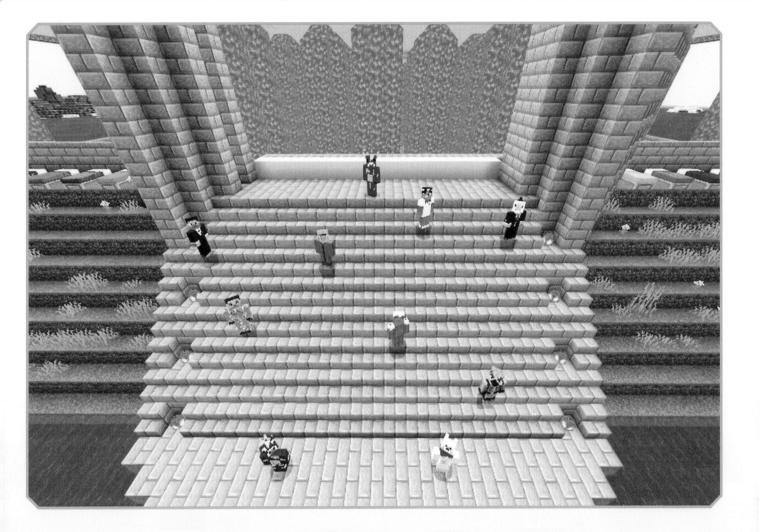

LINK WITH LAN

If you want some multiplayer fun with others who are in the same house or building as you, Minecraft's local area network (LAN) system lets you do this. It's not designed for players to join via the internet. To use the LAN feature, players just have to be on the same network or router, making sure it is visible to others in your settings. As many as four can join together through a LAN.

SELECT A SERVER

The servers tab is where the multiplayer Minecraft world really opens up before you! Choose an online server from the options provided and you'll join others in a fun adventure, which can include multiplayer minigames. All you need is connection to the internet, plus your Xbox Live account. Be sure to **stay safe online** and only join servers that belong to people you trust.

REALMS REVEALED

As official Minecraft servers, Realms are an extremely popular way for minigame makers to share their creations with their friends. Creating a Realm requires a subscription, which you'll need an adult to do for you. However, to play on a friend's Realm map, only that person needs to have the payment set up and others are then free to join in. Realms allow up to ten of your friends to play together at once.

FUN FACT

If you're interested in giving your own Realm a try to see what it's all about, check out Minecraft's 30-day free trial option.

PRICING PLANS – REALMS FOR MINECRAFT: JAVA EDITION

Pick any option below to play with up to 10 friends at the same time!

RECURRING: $7.99 / MONTH

The easiest way to pay: the subscription is automatically extended each month but can be cancelled at any time. It's 20% cheaper than manually buying a 30-day subscription each month.

BUY

ONE TIME CHARGE: 30 DAYS $9.99

This subscription expires after 30 days, so you'll need to log-in and pay again if you want to extend your subscription. However, it's the most expensive way to pay for a Realm.

BUY

ONE TIME CHARGE: 90 DAYS $26.99

This subscription expires after 90 days but can be manually extended if you log-in and pay again. It's 10% cheaper than manually buying a 30-day subscription each month.

BUY

ONE TIME CHARGE: 180 DAYS $47.99

This subscription expires after 180 days but can be manually extended if you log-in and pay again. It's 20% cheaper than manually buying a 30-day subscription each month.

BUY

US prices correct as of 22/9/21

OWN IT

The Realm owner is the only one who can invite others to join and, even when the owner is not online, his or her friends can still have access to it. Remember that Realms are ultimately designed for small groups of friends or family. You'll need to spend time playing with your Realm configuration, through the settings menu. Things like your Realm name, mode, and difficulty setting are key decisions to make.

REALMS PLUS

Realms Plus is a cool monthly subscription service that was launched in 2019. The great thing about it is that players have access to the Marketplace content, where over 100 extras can be picked up, such as community-created skins, texture and mash-up packs, plus adventure maps, and some mega minigames to get you thinking creatively.

SHOW IT OFF

Don't forget to show off your Realm as well, and make it look fun and exciting to your friends. You can do that by taking some stunning screenshots of its top features, then posting these images in your feed for others to view and comment on.

GET CREATIVE

While Survival mode is what most Minecraft fans operate in during general play, when you're tasked with building an adventurous minigame, it can make life much harder! Survival means you must mine your resources, find food, keep a close eye on your hunger and health bar, and deal with the constant threat of mobs. You also need knowledge of crafting and recipes in order to conjure up all the items you will require.

FUN FACT

Mobs still spawn in Creative, but they won't be hostile and attack you while you build your minigame. Phew!

ALL YOU NEED

Thankfully, Creative mode does away with all this. In this setting, your creative inventory gives you access to all the blocks you'll need, so there's no pressure to mine for coal, iron, or even precious diamond ores, for example. Tools, weapons, and armor are also instantly at your fingertips and ready to be used for the situations you set up. You can create minigames in Survival if you want to, but you'll need the resources, recipes and know how, so that you can build what you need.

FLYING HIGH

Besides having infinite resources, another major bonus of Creative is being able to fly through the air. When it comes to building and scoping out your minigames, this is essential because you can place blocks wherever you like. You can also get a sky-high view of what you're constructing and zoom around quickly for a view from any angle. Just double-tap your jump control and you'll be flying for fun.

KNOW YOUR NUMBER

Have an idea of the number of players you want involved with your game. It may be clear from the beginning if, for example, you're designing a player versus player (PvP), where only two go head to head. If it's more of a team game, take some time to consider how many people could participate and the space and features it will need.

EXTRA ENEMIES

If you want to take on mobs as part of your game, then that's totally doable... as long as you're brave and up for the fight! This type of setup is usually called player versus environment (PvE) and it often involves different levels being conquered once enemies are defeated.

BLANK IT OUT

Don't be frightened about starting with a blank canvas. Creating a minigame on a flat, vast Minecraft surface may seem kind of boring, but it means you have no distractions and can put blocks down wherever you like. Keep an idea in your head of how it should work—and don't worry about making mistakes and having to rework stuff.

REMEMBER TO SHARE

Make sure that your minigame is noticed by your friends—you need them to join in, otherwise, it'll be pretty dull! Send an invite to your friends by locating their account after opening the menu. Similarly, if a friend has a game to join, you can get in on the action through the Friends tab.

KEEP IT REAL

While some of your ideas for minigames will be wild and wacky, sticking to what you know can pay off, especially in your early days. Games involving basic principles, like races, mazes, shooting, and navigation, draw on things you're probably already familiar with. Always start with the basics and build from there!

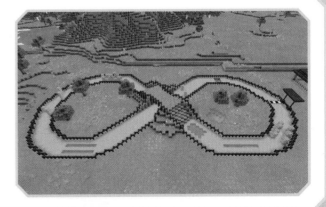

REDSTONE ROCKS!

Learn about the ultra-useful block and item that will bring power to your minigames.

ESSENTIAL STUFF

While new players will need time to become familiar with all the features of Minecraft, one thing that's essential in developing decent minigames is redstone. If you want your Minecraft masterpiece to have moving mechanisms, like in the archery game (pages 20-23) and running the gauntlet (pages 58-61), then you'll need some redstone. This block allows you to create moving parts, and even circuits.

MINING MATTERS

In Creative, you have all the redstone you need. If you're in Survival mode, redstone is commonly found below the surface and mined from blocks of redstone ore. It can be collected using an iron pickaxe, or one of a higher grade. Defeated witch mobs may drop it. It can also be collected from chest loots.

AWESOME USES

Redstone can be used and applied in lots of ways, including lighting, traps, home defense, and automatic doors and farms. In this book, redstone has been specifically used for targets, timers, launchers, hidden exits, and other fun features.

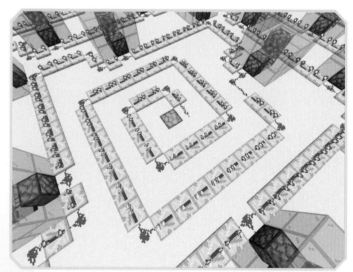

WORD PLAY

The word "redstone" refers to both a block and an item in Minecraft. It can also be connected with anything that's controlled or powered by redstone. This list contains everyday things such as dispensers, pistons, hoppers, and pressure plates.

INSIDER INFO

In these minigame builds, you'll use redstone dust, redstone torches, redstone comparators and redstone repeaters ... here's how they work.

REDSTONE DUST

Dust passes on redstone power when placed down as part of a block.

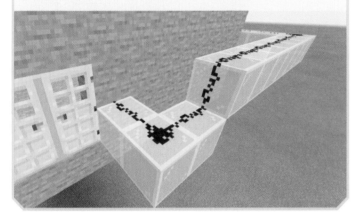

REDSTONE TORCH

A torch will switch redstone power on or off.

REDSTONE COMPARATOR

Comparators form part of redstone circuits to maintain or reduce signal strength.

REDSTONE REPEATER

Repeater blocks are often used to keep redstone power at full capacity.

LET'S GO...

The awesome minigames in this book do not need you to modify your version of Minecraft or search for any special hacks to add. So load up and get set for the games to begin!

AMAZING MAZE

Minecraft is full of a-maze-ing opportunities! Time to build an impressive puzzle where players must choose the right path, or risk getting seriously lost.

MATERIALS

- CONCRETE BLOCKS
- SPRUCE LEAF BLOCKS
- LANTERN BLOCKS
- TORCHES
- WOODEN BLOCKS
- STONE BLOCKS
- ITEM FRAMES
- GLOW ITEM FRAMES
- CHESTS
- SIGN POSTS
- DIAMONDS
- EMERALDS
- JACK O' LANTERNS

STEP 1

Find an interesting or exciting location to build your maze. Here, an area is cleared in a snowy forest, which helps create a mysterious feel. Make sure the space is big enough for your maze plan.

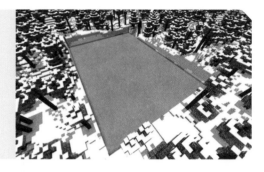

STEP 2

Sketch your design carefully, perhaps using graph paper or an online maze generator. Using a shovel, mark a maze perimeter in the grass and use guidelines to locate the center. Mazes don't have to end in the center, but in this case we will clearly mark a central finishing zone.

STEP 3

Starting at your entrance, begin to mark where your walls will go as you move through. Don't leave any gaps or make confusing mistakes.

STEP 4

Always test your maze route as you build. At this stage, it's a good tip to build a marked route to the finish, shown here by the **orange concrete blocks**.

This orange test path is especially helpful if you are building in Survival mode and not Creative. In Survival, the colored path is your ground route to the finish.

STEP 5

Now you can place the maze walls on the paths you've sketched on the ground. To blend in with the woodland feel, we've used pretty **spruce leaf blocks**.

STEP 6

Build the maze walls at least three blocks high. This means no one can be sneaky and jump over! If walls are only two blocks high, you will be able to jump up and see what's over them.

Building a maze in Creative is much easier since you have the ability to fly and get an aerial view of your construction.

STEP 7

Why not make your central finish zone an attractive place to find? Decorative **stone**, **torches** and **wooden blocks** help to show it off and create a reward for reaching it.

STEP 8

Item frames and **glow item frames** make nice wall displays. **Chests** can also store prizes for players that locate the finish—or a simple place **sign post** shows recognition for their efforts.

Lighting up the finish also identifies it as the area your maze hunters need to reach.

If you want to be generous, you could place helpful signs to show players the way. It's up to you how complex your maze is and how tough it is to crack.

STEP 9

Of course, treats don't have to be hidden right at the finish spot. Try tucking a chest or two in little dead ends on the route, for players who may get lost, or scattering goodies like **diamonds** and **emeralds** to collect.

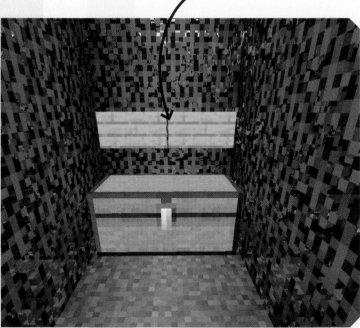

STEP 10

When you're happy with your maze and if you have time, try making it fit well with the scenery. Here, a slope surrounding the perimeter looks very neat.

STEP 11

Don't forget to light up your creation to make it stand out at night. We love these cool **Jack o'Lanterns** placed around the edge!

As a nasty surprise, dangers such as dispensers firing arrows or a lava pit sneakily hidden behind a turn can be built in. Cruel moves, huh?!

ARCHERY

Get ready to take aim as you build a quick-fire archery minigame with arrows, targets and lamps.

MATERIALS

- LEVERS
- REDSTONE DUST
- REDSTONE TORCHES
- REDSTONE REPEATERS
- STICKY PISTON BLOCKS
- TARGET BLOCKS
- STAIR BLOCKS
- REDSTONE LAMPS
- GRASS BLOCKS
- FENCING
- DARK OAK BLOCKS
- BOWS AND ARROWS

Find a flat area to build your archery game. Dig a trench two blocks wide, two blocks deep and 21 blocks long.

At the player end of the trench, add any single block and a **lever** on top. Place a **redstone torch** on the inner side, like this.

STEP 3

Place 18 **redstone repeaters** away from the torch and 18 **redstone repeaters** back toward the lever.

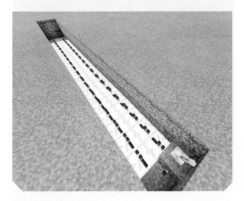

STEP 4

Move the control on the **redstone repeater**, then set it to the maximum time of four ticks. The two visible parts on the **redstone repeater** should be positioned furthest apart. Do this for all **redstone repeaters**.

STEP 5

At the far end, place **redstone dust** to complete the circuit and make an automatic timer. Adjust the tick speed for a shorter timer. For example, one tick is 3.6 seconds and four equals 14.4 seconds.

STEP 6

With the **lever** and **redstone torch** in place, a redstone pulse is continually sent around the circuit. It will only stop when the **lever** is manually pulled to off.

STEP 7

At the end opposite the **lever**, join another line of **redstone dust** to the circuit. Make sure this climbs two blocks to ground level.

STEP 8

Place five **sticky pistons** along the **redstone dust**, making sure they touch it. Now put a **target block** on each **sticky piston block**. These will lift when the pulse travels through the **redstone dust**.

STEP 9

Build nice-looking housing to decorate around the **target blocks**. Put **stair blocks** in, so you can collect the arrows. The housing should be two blocks high to hide the target block when the **sticky piston** is down.

STEP 10

Across the top, leave a one block gap to place a **redstone lamp** above each target block.

STEP 11

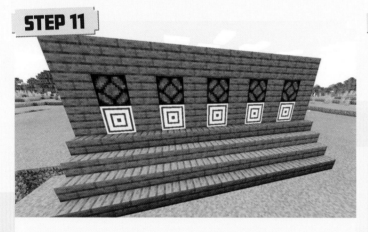

When a **target block** is hit with an **arrow** while it's touching the **redstone lamp**, it will light up.

STEP 12

Now camouflage your circuit (we used **grass blocks** here) and **fence** off the target zone. Place the **fence** far enough away to make the minigame challenging!

STEP 13

Keep the **lever** uncovered and mark it with a **sign post**. Finally, place your own housing to hide the circuit behind the target area. **Dark oak** is used here.

EXTRA TARGET PRACTICE

STEP 14

To the side, **fence** off another area and place **target blocks** with a **redstone lamp** on top. Here, the blocks are arranged at distances of 10, 20, 30 and 50 from the firing spot. **Arrows** have a maximum range of 52 blocks, depending on the angle at which they're fired and the flatness of the land.

STEP 15

Practice hitting the **target blocks** and lighting up the **lamps**. Add **signs** if you feel like making it more fun.

STEP 16

On the other side of your main minigame, place **redstone lamps** in a line (ideally 14). Now put a block of your choice at the end, with a **target block** on top.

STEP 17

Place any blocks behind the **redstone lamps,** so that they are touching. **Redstone dust** runs on these blocks.

STEP 18

Fire an **arrow** at the **target block**. Depending where it's hit, the **redstone lamps** will light up. Striking the center of the target will see all the lamps illuminate.

STEP 19

Fence off the game how you like. Your complete archery minigame arena can be decorated now to look glitzy and cool for other players to join in. It'll look awesome at night, too, with the lamps being triggered!

OBSTACLE COURSE

Test your skill, timing and bravery by taking on an obstacle course minigame. Building one is fun, then trying it out with friends is even more of a blast.

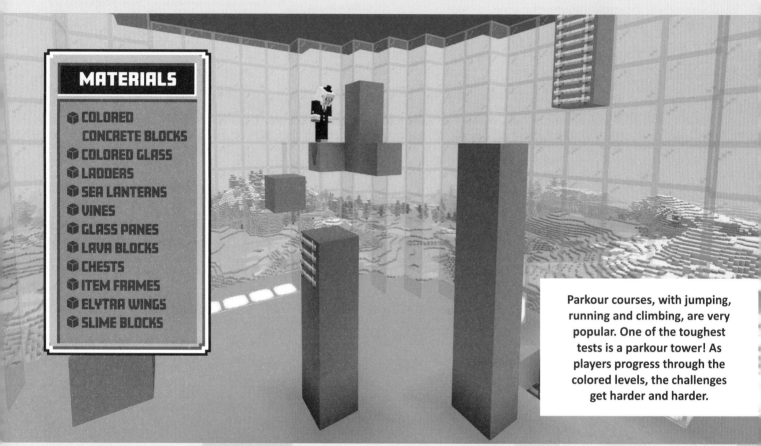

MATERIALS

- COLORED CONCRETE BLOCKS
- COLORED GLASS
- LADDERS
- SEA LANTERNS
- VINES
- GLASS PANES
- LAVA BLOCKS
- CHESTS
- ITEM FRAMES
- ELYTRA WINGS
- SLIME BLOCKS

Parkour courses, with jumping, running and climbing, are very popular. One of the toughest tests is a parkour tower! As players progress through the colored levels, the challenges get harder and harder.

STEP 1

Use **concrete blocks** to form the base of each level and the obstacles, with **colored glass** creating each section.

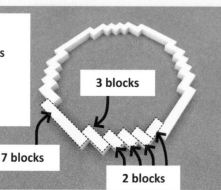

Follow these measurements and repeat to complete the circle.

3 blocks

7 blocks

2 blocks

STEP 2

Make sure each story is high enough for the obstacle activities you have planned. Each colored parkour tower section can vary in height.

STEP 3

At ground level, it's very simple. Obstacles are built with single gaps and single block jump heights. The **red concrete blocks** here contrast with the **glass** tower. An obstacle color closer to the tower's color would make it a little trickier.

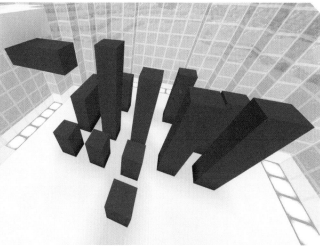

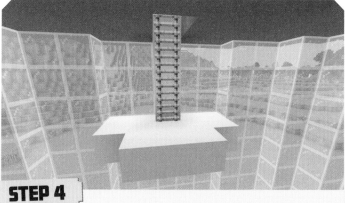

STEP 4

Moving between the levels is achieved by the **ladders**. This is easy to do, but be creative—maybe you'll use **vines** or **pistons** instead as a way to move up to the next section of your tower?

STEP 5

It's important to light the levels, so that you can see what you're doing. This build uses plenty of **sea lanterns**, which are an excellent light source.

STEP 6

On the next level, increase the jumping difficulty ever so slightly. Here, we have placed more diagonal jumps and some gaps that stretch two blocks. This is still no real test for most players!

STEP 7

At the green level, the variation of block height and gaps is increased again.

STEP 8

Remember that a player can usually jump over a maximum of a four-block gap, or three blocks with a height rise of one block.

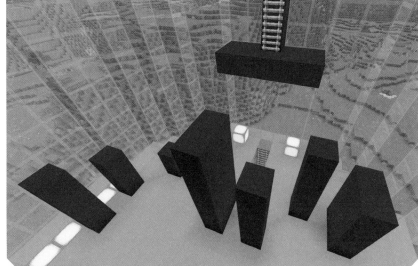

STEP 9

Notice how in this yellow stage and on the previous green base, things are made tougher by reducing the size of the landing platform around the escape **ladder**. A more precise leap is needed!

STEP 10

You can begin to see the step up in difficulty on the yellow base parkour. Keyboard or controller skills are definitely starting to be tested!

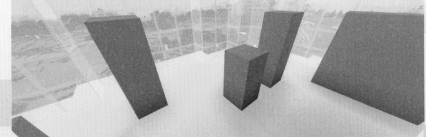

STEP 11

Let's really give the obstacle course a big degree of difficulty with some corner gaps. At times, this means players need to jump forward from their obstacle, with the aim of strafing (moving sideways) to land on a block around the corner.

STEP 12

See how the orange parkour platform introduces four-block gaps to navigate. Jumping these requires good timing.

STEP 13

Watch out—the red level represents danger! **Glass panes** present a real challenge because they are much thinner than regular blocks. Landing on them requires complete concentration, although players can still run across and leap from these panes.

STEP 14

Make life more difficult by placing more **glass**—they can be a real "pane" for parkour fans!

STEP 15

The **ladder** now has no platform below or to the side of it. One false leap and you won't make it.

STEP 16

Time to think pink, folks. With this arrangement, a player must know how to jump on the spot, sprint immediately on contact and then jump almost immediately to gain the speed and height needed to hit the next obstacle. This takes practice.

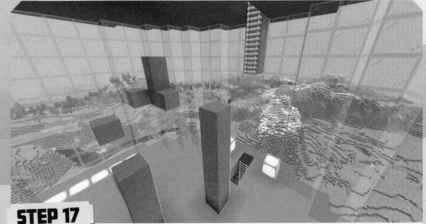

STEP 17

This level may seem daunting, but if your players want a test, then this degree of difficulty should be added. You don't want players to become bored or finish the tower too quickly!

STEP 18

Notice how a **ladder** is also used on this block during the course and not just at the exit platform.

STEP 19

Think of how difficult your final parkour platform can be. We have installed **lava blocks**, which is about as mean as you can be!

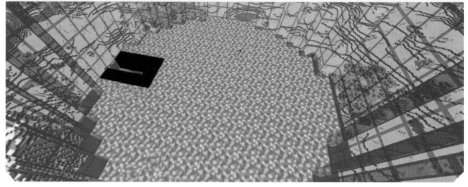

STEP 20

All of the final obstacles are **glass panes**. The margin of error now is very small—one little slip and it's lethal lava time.

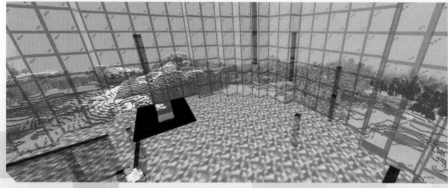
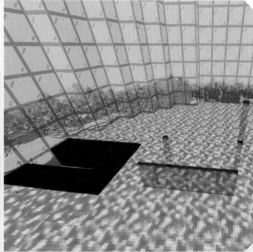

STEP 21

Now relax at the very top of the tower, once all obstacles have been mastered. In this build, a prize room is used as a reward for those skilled enough to get there.

STEP 22

Chests and **item frames** can offer cool rewards. You don't need to do this, but it's a great incentive and a nice surprise.

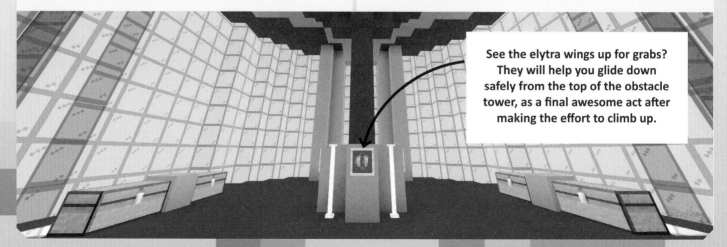

See the elytra wings up for grabs? They will help you glide down safely from the top of the obstacle tower, as a final awesome act after making the effort to climb up.

STEP 23

Plus, there's an area of **slime blocks** to aim for on the ground as you bravely leap from this gigantic tower of games. Good luck on the way up... and on the way down!

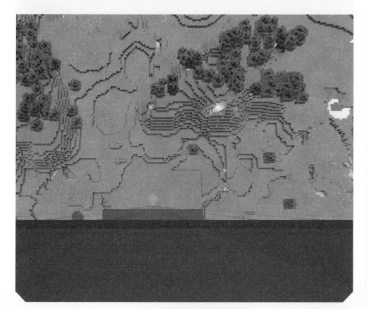

STEP 24

You can also use some **colored glass** blocks to create a fun and welcoming entrance to your parkour tower!

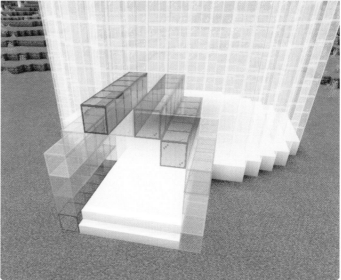

ANIMAL RACE

The next three minigames are all about racing and competing.
Let's kick off with a crazy and cool pig-running track!

MATERIALS

- PIGS
- WOODEN BLOCKS
- FENCING
- GATES
- WOODEN SLABS
- GRASS BLOCKS
- DIRT BLOCKS
- BLACK BLOCKS
- WHITE BLOCKS
- TORCHES
- HAY BALES
- JACK O' LANTERNS
- WATER BLOCKS

STEP 1

For a land-based racing and track
minigame, you can rely on the
trusty **pig**. These cute creatures
can be saddled up and raced
against your friends—just as long
as you dangle a carrot on a stick to
keep them moving!

STEP 2

Select a nice flat area that's large
enough to stage the track design
you want. You can make it as big as
you want—but keeping it simple
and quite small at first makes
sense and will suit the little piggies.

STEP 3

Before you create the race arena, you need a pigpen to look after your animals. Begin to build this to the side of where your track will be.

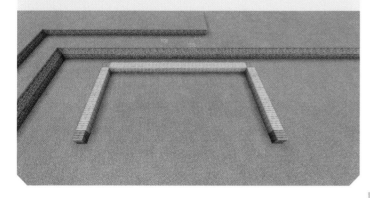

STEP 4

Use **wooden blocks** or whichever blocks you like. Here, we have built the walls, used a decorative **fence** and added a **gate** as an entrance and exit.

STEP 5

A nice roof makes the pen more comfortable for the pigs. Remember that these farm animals are the stars of this event, so make them as happy as possible!

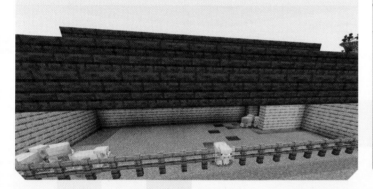

STEP 6

This racing track design is called a figure eight. It's a classic shape, is fun to make and doesn't need too much space.

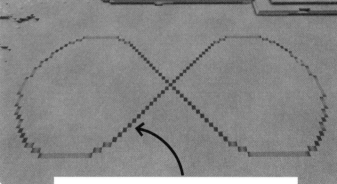

Mark it out in the grass using a shovel. The rectangular area after the straight section is the start and finish zone.

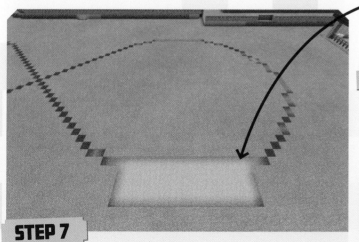

STEP 7

A track that's five or six blocks wide is perfect for a race against a handful of other **pigs** and riders.

STEP 8

From your design, begin to build out the track to the width you want. You will have both curves and straight sections to create.

STEP 9

Where the track intersects, try making a structure to act as a bridge and a tunnel, so that the **pigs** don't collide there. Riders will race under it one way, then over it the other way.

STEP 10

Wooden slabs make a path for the pigs to climb and **wooden blocks** bridge the gap to the other side.

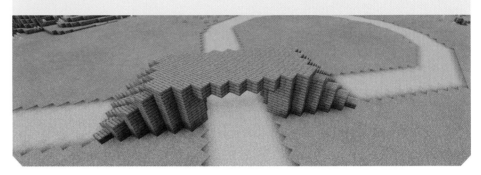

STEP 11

If you want to make the bridge look more natural, build up **dirt** and **grass** around each side. Make it as decorative as you want.

STEP 12

With the track in place, think about adding a perimeter **fence** on the inside and outside to keep the riders in the right place. Pigs can't walk over **fence posts** and this option looks good against the surroundings.

Pigs can walk over single blocks, though. So, if you use another material as a fence, just make sure it's high enough to pen your animals in.

STEP 13

At the start and finish zone, make a raised structure and an entrance for the riders. It'll give this part of the track extra importance. You can be as extravagant as you want with the build.

STEP 14

At this stage, some **torches** or other light sources will look attractive and help you to use the track at night. Across your track, add in a black and white line to act as the spot to begin and end a race.

STEP 15

To ramp up the racing difficulty, put down some obstacles for the **pigs** to pass through. **Hay bales** are perfect. **Jack o'Lanterns** are great, too, because they will light the way.

STEP 16

Other obstacles and tests to place on the track include dips and **water** hazards. These could be at narrow places in the track and create a hazard for the riders to force their way through.

Be as creative as you want with the track. Use trees and flowers to enhance the landscape, or perhaps even build a second pigpen.

BOAT RACE

Now you really are launching off on a wacky race course. Take to the water and "sea" what challenges await you!

MATERIALS

- WOODEN BLOCKS
- FENCING
- BOATS
- WOODEN STAIRS
- COLORED WOOL BLOCKS
- MOB EGGS
- LILY PADS
- CORAL BLOCKS
- BLACK BLOCKS
- MAGMA BLOCKS

Fun, adventure, surprises... a boat race can pack a lot in. After finding this interesting strip of coastline, we set up a circuit there to take advantage of the islands and natural features. Choose wherever interests you in your world.

STEP 1

Start by placing a deck as a launch base for the boats. This build has a classic wooden style, with **fences** and **stairs** to the water. The steps help with entering and exiting the boats. Put a range of **colored boats** down next to the deck.

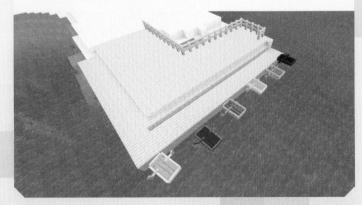

STEP 2

Create a starting line close to the deck. We have a decorative arch for ours, with enough space for the racers to line up.

STEP 3

You can see how our boat racetrack is beginning to take shape. It uses **white wool**, which stands out against the water, but feel free to make use of any color or pattern you want.

The track markings are kept at the water level. This lets racers take in the stunning scenery, as well as keep an eye on other boats in the event.

STEP 4

Add in turns and obstacles to challenge competitors. Use the ideas here if they help you map out a cool course.

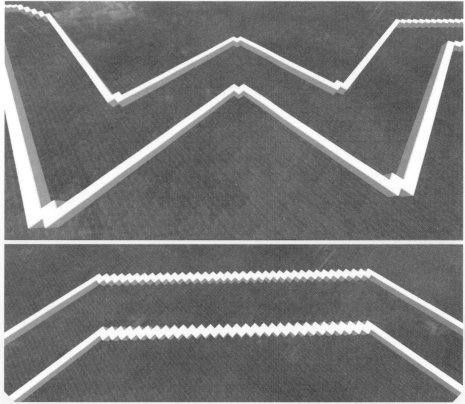

STEP 5

Use the natural obstacles already on the water, such as small islands and rock bases. This saves on your building resources, if you are in Survival, and provides a natural look.

STEP 6

Will you plan the route before you start, or just go with the flow and see what happens once you build? Either way will work. Take an aerial view to see the overall picture.

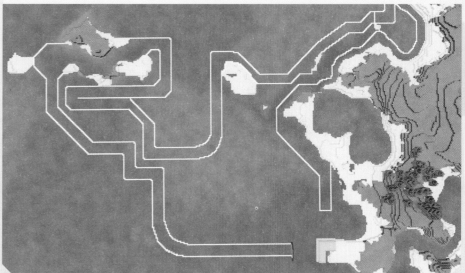

STEP 8

Next, think about the hazards you may want to introduce. In Creative, you can place any of the available **mob eggs** to spawn enemies. Check out these skeleton archers, which will definitely slow racers down!

See how these umbrella-like structures on the water protect the mobs from burning in sunlight.

STEP 7

Doubling back on your route and sharing walls will also save on resources and time. Add in long straights, twisted sections and tight bends.

STEP 9

Explore the idea of building **lily pads**. They will give the boat drivers another obstacle to navigate—they break when touched, but slow people down. How about a time penalty for destroying them?

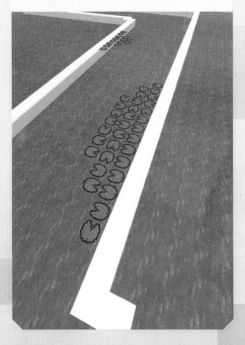

STEP 10

Coral blocks, lurking just above the surface, look pretty and force drivers to dodge them.

STEP 11

Extra short walls, coming away from the side of the track, will make players fight over space as they try to race through. Walls running parallel to the track will also force decisions to be made. Any kind of bottleneck just ramps up the tension!

STEP 12

Think about placing **magma blocks** under the water. The rising bubbles will shake boats on the surface. This type of hazard is very difficult to detect, too.

STEP 13

If your water track is not in a loop design, then add in a finish line or arch as well. Place down any decorations you want, and perhaps **signs** or other helpful items along the route.

STEP 14

We love this added final touch of pixel art as an awesome coastline attraction. Make your course a fun place to be and a first-class racing spectacle!

SKY RACE

Get up in the clouds and speed through the gates and obstacles... the race is on and the sky's the limit!

MATERIALS

- COLORED BLOCKS
- LADDERS
- SLIME BLOCKS
- STAINED GLASS
- ELYTRA WINGS
- FIREWORK ROCKETS
- CHESTS
- STICKY PISTON BLOCKS
- BUTTONS
- REDSTONE DUST
- REDSTONE REPEATERS
- WATER BLOCKS
- SWITCHES
- TRIPWIRE
- BEDS
- DISPENSERS
- FENCES

STEP 1

Choose a tower shape that catches your eye, either traditional or a bit fantastical. Building upward in Creative is much easier; however, this can be done in Survival, too, with the help of scaffolding.

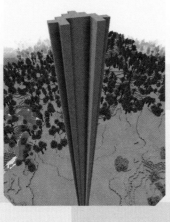

STEP 2

Ladders are in place from the base to the very top, while **slime blocks** are built in to soften anyone's fall.

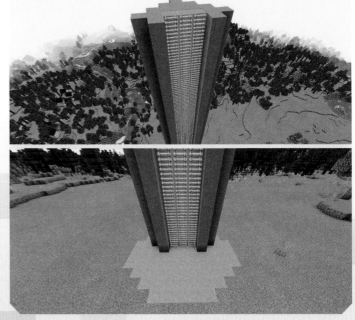

We're building a sky-high tower to give us the height for racing and a great view out. The layout is simple yet challenging enough to tempt a competition between players.

STEP 3

At the top is a staging room for our flying racers. This is a simple circular room with **stained glass**. Use any blocks you want to design your own according to your taste.

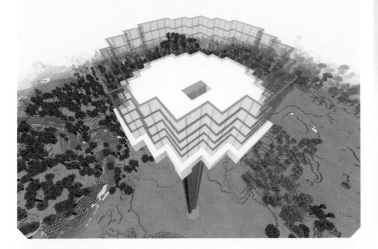

STEP 4

The ceiling will serve as the floor of your launch pad. The pad needs to be a good size and may need to be extended out over the base below it.

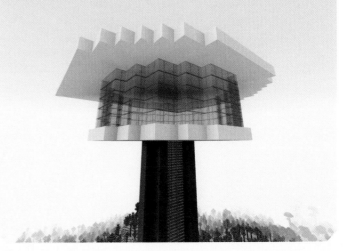

STEP 5

Fill your staging zone with any items and goodies you may want, which must include plenty of **elytra wings** and **firework rockets** for your racing players. Here, a **ladder** takes visitors up to the launch pad.

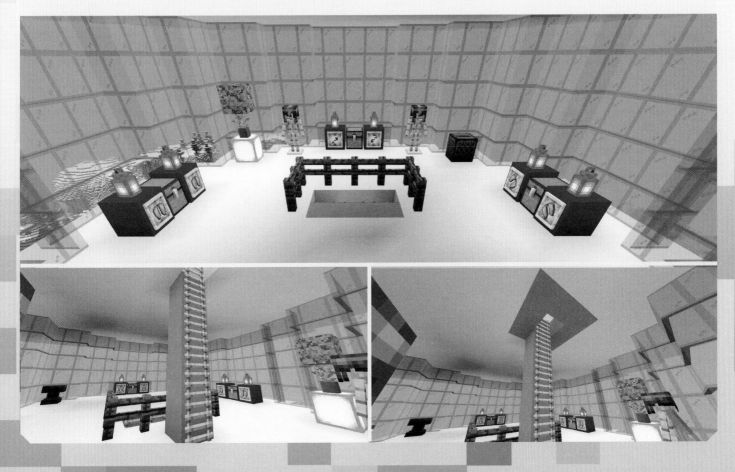

STEP 6

One end of the launch zone has a starting platform. Lay down **sticky pistons**, leaving a one-block gap in front of them.

Place a **slime block** on each. This is where players stand to be launched into the air, so don't obstruct the area above it!

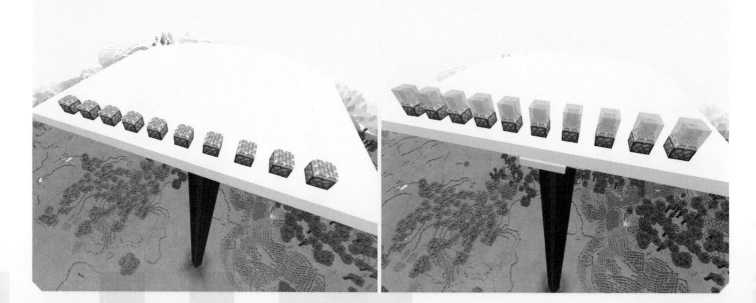

STEP 7

Place a block aligning with the **sticky pistons** on a direct diagonal—not in front or to the side. Put a **button** on this block, then use **redstone dust** to lay a wire from underneath it to all of the pistons. The signal may need extending with a **repeater**, as we have done.

A push on the button launches players a few blocks high, all at the same time.

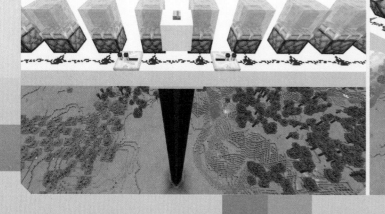

STEP 8

Decorate the starting platform. Any blocks directly touching the front, rear or sides of the **slime block** will be pushed or pulled with it, when it is moved by a **sticky piston**. Here, the **purple blocks** will lift up. Do not put any structures, such as **fences** or **switches**, on them.

STEP 9

Now begin to construct the gates that flyers navigate through as they race the track. These circular gates are 15 blocks wide.

STEP 11

Have your first racing gate quite near to your start platform. Each gate should be clearly visible from the one before it. Make them bigger and cover a large distance if you wish—remember that **elytra** is powerful!

STEP 10

One side is green to show that a player is moving in the correct direction, and the other is red, which means they are not. This traffic light system should be simple to follow.

STEP 12

Keep the path of the gates simple to test a player's sky-racing speed—or vary the angles and direction as a test of flying agility. Changing direction and making players dive is all part of the fun.

STEP 13

The Minecraft Overworld generates a lot of awesome shapes and structures. You could take advantage of this and add these features to your track, like we did in the boat race. Watch out for natural gates that could be included or marked out on your route.

STEP 14

Feel like flying through a mountain, instead of just up and over it? Tunnel through one and make it part of your race, adding gate markings and even a drop of lava for extra pressure.

STEP 15

When you're happy with the sky-racing track, build a landing area and finish line. Ours is part way up the tower on the opposite side to the launch pad.

Make it any shape you like but use a shallow angle to allow players to land safely. Ours has a long platform with a pool of water. Water can provide a safe touchdown, but is also a hazard as a player aims to cross the finish line quickly.

STEP 16

Another idea for a finish line uses **dispensers** and **tripwire**. Place a **dispenser**, facing upward, and fill it with **fireworks**. You can have a variation of **switches** to make these launch, but we have **tripwire** between two **dispensers** at our finish.

STEP 17

Add **beds** as a spawn point at the launch site for those unlucky enough to fall to the ground. Remember to bring in some cool illuminations for night-time racing, too. Get ready for lots of sky-high action!

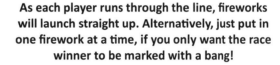

As each player runs through the line, fireworks will launch straight up. Alternatively, just put in one firework at a time, if you only want the race winner to be marked with a bang!

ARENA

Arenas are perfect for player versus player (PvP) action. Check out this smart but simple build for a fun team battle.

MATERIALS

- STONE BLOCKS
- BEDS
- IRON DOORS
- PRESSURE PLATES
- COLORED BLOCKS
- BANNERS
- WOODEN BLOCKS
- GLOW ITEM FRAMES
- WEAPONS
- ARMOR
- POTIONS
- END RODS

STEP 1

Choose any location you want for an arena build, but a flat stretch of land, perhaps by a clearing in a forest area, will look quite dramatic.

STEP 2

Build a circle like this. The diameter is 25 blocks. Building with an odd number of blocks such as this means that the center is one block wide. So, if you want to place a door in the middle spot, it will be exactly in the center.

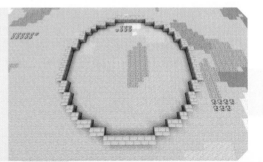

STEP 3

See how the rest of the floor uses **decorative stones**. Use any materials you want, but spend some time to make your base quite eye-catching because that is where the conquests will take place.

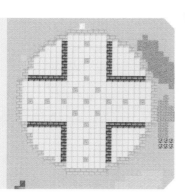

STEP 4

Using the **stone** lines created, place four arena bases on the edges of the circular shape. They will be spawn areas for the players or teams.

Make them big enough to house whatever equipment you want inside, which includes a bed to serve as the spawn point.

STEP 5

Each of the four bases can be any shape, but it's probably best to keep them all the same.

STEP 6

On the outside, include an **iron door** with a **pressure plate** to allow external entrance. **Iron doors** are strong and can't catch fire.

Pressure plate

STEP 7

This is your base before you enter the arena. We suggest making each of the four a different color—one is shown here made with **blue concrete blocks**, with a **bed**. Team colors can also be on display outside your external door as **banners**.

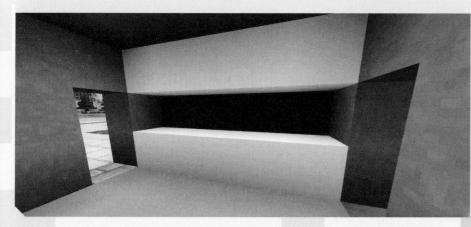

Blue banner

STEP 8

Use **concrete** and **wood blocks** to your taste to create an awesome look. There's storage space here and **glow item frames** proudly show off the items available for your quest. Choose from things like a **sword**, **armor** and **potions**.

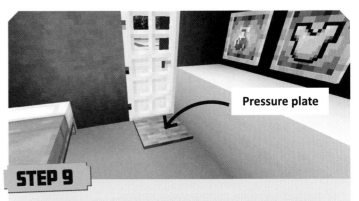

Pressure plate

If the game is set up with multiple rounds, then you should think about adding spare equipment.

STEP 9

Include another **pressure plate** on the inside of another **iron door**, which opens to the arena. It means that when a player or team leaves this base, if they are eliminated or killed in the arena, they will then respawn inside the base. The door will not open from the arena side.

STEP 10

You can see how the other arena bases begin to look. Red, green and purple have been used.

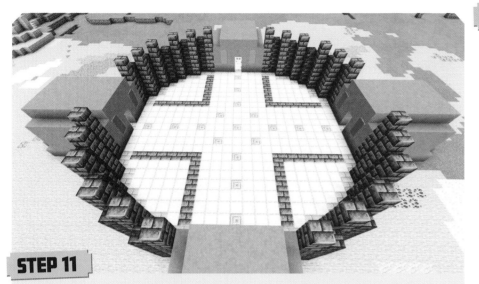

STEP 12

Some gentle landscaping will help—maybe a few plants and trees, and definitely some light sources to give it a night-time glow. We have used **end rods**.

STEP 11

Obviously, you need to build strong walls around the arena, between each of the bases. **Decorative stones** provide a historical feel, while adding toughness.

After you have experienced the arena and adapted your build, perhaps with extra spawn points for a team tussle, you can begin to decorate the outside area.

CAPTURE THE FLAG

Fancy more PvP battle fun? Capture the flag is always a big hit, either between single players or larger teams. Discover how to set up the scene.

MATERIALS

- STONE BRICK BLOCKS
- STAINED GLASS
- BEDS
- STONE BLOCKS
- STAIR BLOCKS
- FENCING
- BANNERS
- WOODEN BLOCKS
- WATER BLOCKS
- HAY BALES
- DARK OAK BLOCKS
- DIRT BLOCKS
- TREES
- VINES

STEP 1

Choose your space to build. For simplicity, this arena is on a flat surface and the playing zone is enclosed, but you may decide on an open area to increase the tension.

STEP 2

In keeping with the historical feel of our capture the flag game, **stone brick** has been used to build high walls in a large rectangular shape.

We have gone for a simple set up that features two teams, a symmetrical map, color coordination, and respawn points on each side.

Capture the flag (CTF) is a game where two teams compete to capture the opposing team's flag. The first team to capture the other team's flag and bring it safely back to their own base wins.

STEP 3

Each team end needs to be distinctive to the players. This build uses a cool **stained glass** artwork feature in the team's chosen color.

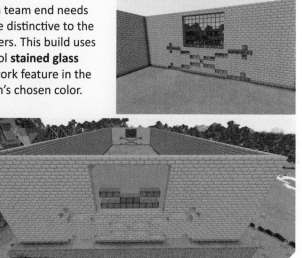

STEP 4

The team's base tower will be built to the side of the artwork. It uses a semicircle design backed against the wall. This will act as the spawn base.

STEP 5

Begin to build up your base tower from the ground. You want the height to help protect you and to limit spawn kills. Spawn kills happen when a player respawns, but an enemy player is standing right there for an instant elimination—super annoying!

STEP 6

Each player on a team needs a **bed** placed in their tower, which will be the spawn point.

Storage for equipment has also been added to the top of the tower, in the form of chests and barrels. Consider adding extra height or stories to your build. This is your home, so make it as exciting (or fearsome!) as you want.

STEP 7

Begin to jazz up your base. This build uses more **decorative stones** to enhance the castle turret look—see the lookout spots on the top, which help to observe advancing enemies on the ground.

Of course, stairs are crucial to give you access to the top level. They don't need to go directly all the way to the top, though, and could instead lead you to a middle level, which would then have internal steps up.

STEP 8

Spend a little time thinking about the objective of your flag game. In our game, the winning player or team is the first to capture all three flags that are hanging in your opponent's area.

STEP 9

This basic **stone** platform, positioned just outside the base, makes a great stage to display the three flags. You'll notice that the flags are actually banners, which look very effective in this setting.

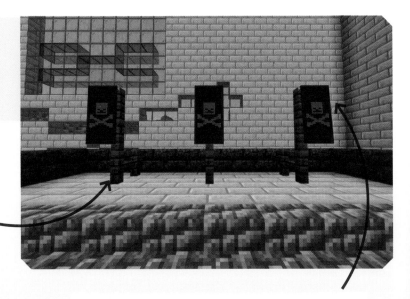

There are a variety of blocks you can use to show off your flags. A crimson fencepost does a good job here since it looks like a red flagpole.

Use a loom to create your own pattern and design on your team's banners (flags). You may like to match the colors and shapes to those on your team's wall.

STEP 10

Next is the important step of placing obstacles on the terrain between each team's base and flag platform. These features are essential—otherwise, there are no cover or environmental features to hide behind and launch surprise attacks.

STEP 11

In our flag game, a shed-like outbuilding, water feature, natural hump and another platform are included. Add in what captures your imagination and try to tie it in with the game's overall theme.

Paths, trees, foliage, and overgrowth can be added in at this stage.

STEP 12

Since we have chosen a symmetrical game, what we've placed on this side of the arena should also be built on the other side. Look at how the features match in our build.

The build does not have to match on each side. If you want more buildings and features for cover on just one side, then that will suit a game style that's based on more attack-defend tactics.

STEP 13

Check out the red and blue entrances built on either side of the center line. Make these as decorative as you want.

Add lighting for some intense night-time raids, because hunting for those famous flags doesn't stop once daylight disappears. Enjoy the battle, folks!

How about a central feature across the middle line, just like this water area? It could create chaotic—but fun!—scenes in the race for the flags. Just make sure it doesn't obscure too much of each side or block the view of the flag platform to any great extent.

If you're feeling brave, include a mob as something else to contend with, as you seek out the flags belonging to the other team!

BATTLE ROYALE

Battle royale games attract plenty of players, so here's a fun-looking build to create a great base for an action-packed adventure.

MATERIALS

- COLORED BLOCKS
- PISTON BLOCKS
- GLASS BLOCKS
- LAVA BLOCKS
- REDSTONE TORCHES
- REDSTONE REPEATERS
- REDSTONE DUST
- STICKY PISTON BLOCKS
- TREES AND PLANTS
- BEDS
- STONE FENCING
- DIAMOND PICKAXE
- DISPENSER BLOCKS
- LEVERS
- OBSIDIAN BLOCK
- SHROOM LIGHTS
- IRON DOORS

STEP 1

Find an area to build your base or set one up, like the one here. Our optimum base size is 51 by 51 blocks, so the island is 60 by 60 blocks to allow for that. Then, make a zone that's four blocks deep, so that once a player enters in, they can't escape very easily.

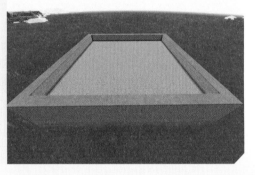

STEP 2

Place a ceiling over it that's the same size as the arena below it. Lava will fall in from here. Leaving a one-block gap from the perimeter, place single block holes with a seven-block space between them. Carefully repeat the hole pattern so they are halfway between the horizontal and vertical gaps.

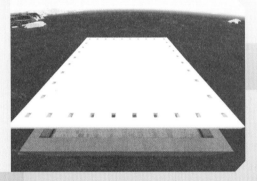

The aim of a battle royale quest is to set up a hostile battle zone, then make players retreat to a fighting area in the center that's continually decreasing.

Using the magic of redstone, the idea is that lava drops in from high up, forcing players to a certain area as the minigame ticks on. It's fun but frantic!

STEP 3

Mark out the holes in a diagonal grid way, leaving a good-sized gap in the middle.

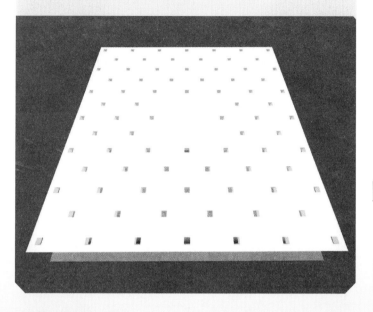

STEP 4

You now need a **piston** next to each hole, which has the job of exposing the hole when it is not powered. Keep the **piston** facing outward and with the back toward the middle of the ceiling.

STEP 5

Place **glass blocks** around each hole, creating a place where **lava blocks** can be stored a block above the hole. This means that the lava can flow through when the piston's unpowered. When the **piston** is powered, the lava is blocked from dropping to the island below.

STEP 6

This process needs to be repeated for all of the holes, as shown here. It will take a little time so be patient.

STEP 7

Now they require connecting in a circuit. A **redstone torch** will keep them powered while laying the circuit.

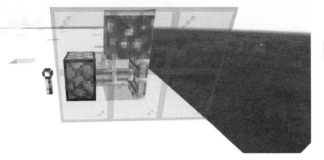

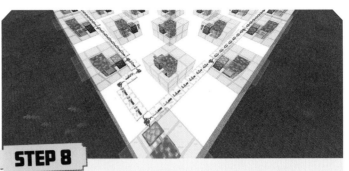

STEP 8

Place **redstone repeaters** around the perimeter of the first ring of lava traps. Position a single **redstone dust** behind each **piston**, in place of a **repeater**, so that it can be powered.

STEP 9

Complete the circuit around the outer edge, then do the same behind the next ring of **lava blocks**. Do this until all of the lava traps have been wired like so.

Repeaters will decide the rate that the lava falls. Each can be set from 0.1 to 0.4 seconds. The spacing here between the traps creates a lag of between 0.7 to 2.8 seconds from each lava deposit. A bigger build can extend this time, so play around with your design.

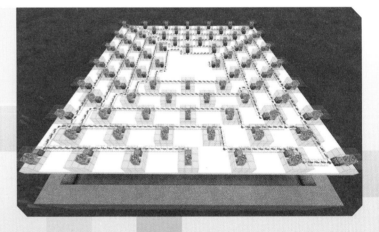

STEP 10

The circuit will eventually spiral inward to the center block, where we have placed a **dispenser block** facing down toward the arena. The dispenser's purpose is revealed later!

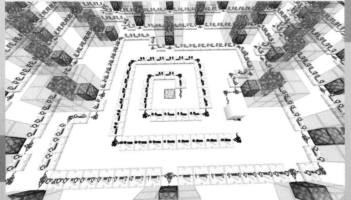

STEP 11

Feed the circuit into a block with a **redstone torch** on the other side of it. Now position a **redstone dust** that feeds to another repeater circuit, coming away from the side with the **redstone torch**.

STEP 12

While the lava traps are powered, the circuit in the middle won't power because of the **redstone torch**. As soon as the final part of the circuit does lose power, the **redstone torch** gains its power back and will begin the timer for the **dispenser**.

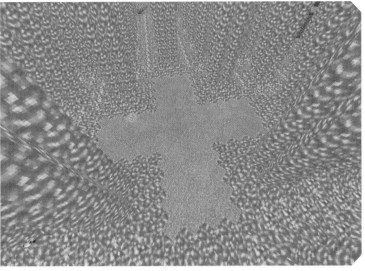

STEP 13

Check out this impressive starting platform and notice the block with **lever** and **redstone torch**. This torch is the main power supply to the circuits. Keep the power on, but once a player uses the lever to switch it off, the **pistons** in the lava traps deactivate and the scary hot stuff begins to flow!

STEP 14

However, you don't want the traps to activate straight away. Make a delay by building a ring around the island, which starts at the **redstone torch**, with as many **redstone repeaters** as you like.

STEP 15

Wire it up to the circuit in the roof using **glass blocks**. Now all the traps will keep closed while they are powered.

STEP 16

Place another **torch** on the **lever** block, which will power a gate that lowers when the lever's flipped. Run a line of **redstone dust** from the **torch** to a row of **sticky pistons**. The **sticky pistons** need to be powered, so that they are raised. The top part of the **sticky piston** should be exposed above our platform's level.

STEP 17

Put a block on each **sticky piston**, so that it's now two blocks in total above the base. This means players can't jump over it to reach the arena—they need to wait until the **lever** is hit and the power to both circuits is stopped. Then, the gate lowers and players can access.

The timer circuit will lose power at the same time, gradually losing power to all the lava traps. When a game is done, just switch the lever to raise the gate, block the lava traps and reset the battle royale.

STEP 18

When you're happy that the circuits work well, begin to hide them all. Here, pillars and grass slopes fit well, but make sure not to disturb or break any circuits when you hide them.

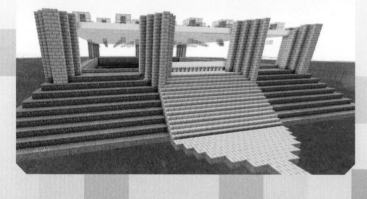

STEP 19

See how the ceiling structure can also be covered how you want. **Plants** and **trees** fit the island theme very well.

STEP 20

The **beds** are spawn points for when players are eliminated from the intense action in the arena.

The arena border now has a fence as well, ensuring access is blocked, apart from at the correct points. We used a wooden fence but, after it caught fire, we switched to stone!

STEP 21

Remember the **dispenser** you placed? Put a **diamond pickaxe** in there so that, during the final battle, the power in the central circuit will make it drop to the floor. It can then be used to smash a block of **obsidian** in the center of the arena, so the remaining player can exit!

STEP 22

Under the **obsidian block**, there can be a fancy room for the final player to explore. **Shroom lights** in the floor will light the way, and adding a tunnel back to the platform is a good idea. At the end of the tunnel, an **iron door** with a one-way switch means the winner can exit.

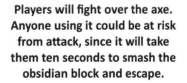

Players will fight over the axe. Anyone using it could be at risk from attack, since it will take them ten seconds to smash the obsidian block and escape.

Try building structures in the battle royale arena for players to camp out around. Loot items will also raise the stakes and represent a threat for those taking part in the game.

THE GAUNTLET

This is a straightforward way to build a cool "survival valley" game, where one wrong step means you're out. Running the gauntlet is never easy!

MATERIALS

- COLORED BLOCKS
- DISPENSER BLOCKS
- REDSTONE DUST
- REDSTONE COMPARATORS
- GLASS BLOCKS
- REDSTONE REPEATERS
- PRESSURE PLATES
- POLISHED BLACKSTONE BLOCKS
- STONE BLOCKS

STEP 1

To make the long corridor needed, build two walls that are three blocks high. You can then see how wide your gauntlet valley will be.

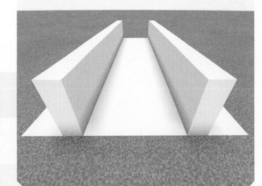

STEP 2

Place **dispenser** blocks, which will eventually connect to **redstone**, along the top of each wall. Then, remove your corridor wall blocks, like this.

To make it simpler to see each step of this build, this minigame is being created on a flat surface in Creative. The idea is that redstone under the valley's floor will fire arrows, or another danger, at a player from a dispenser. The only way to navigate through is by avoiding the hidden danger.

STEP 3

Redstone dust now needs to be placed horizontally along the corridor. See how there's a one-block gap of **redstone dust** in each strip. This forms the safe passage a player must find.

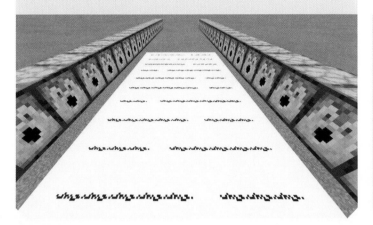

STEP 4

Next up is creating the circuit. Feed the **redstone dust** into the back of a **redstone comparator**, setting it to subtract. The light on the **comparator** shows it is in this mode.

Make a one-block loop of redstone, leaving the redstone comparator and going back into the side. This forms a circuit that will switch itself off and on in a rapid fashion, as long as it's powered.

STEP 5

In this minigame, **glass blocks** are used to carry the **redstone** signal from the ground and up into the back of the **dispenser**. Use a **redstone repeater** if needed, to ensure that power can reach each **dispenser**.

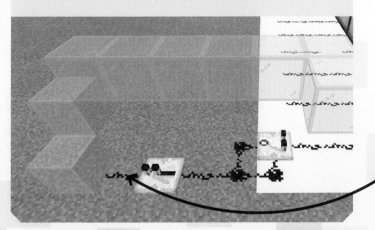

Have more redstone dust coming away, which will eventually connect to the back of each dispenser block.

STEP 6

Place a block above the **redstone dust** and then a **pressure plate** on that block. This acts as the trigger to feed into the **dispenser**, meaning that when a player steps on a block that's wired up, they come under attack from whatever shoots from the **dispenser**!

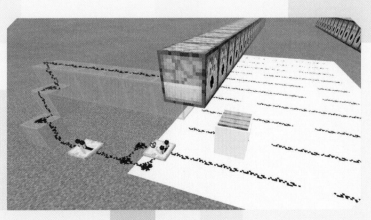

STEP 7

The whole of the valley's floor needs blocks and **pressure plates**. **Polished blackstone** is used here, which is a good tip if you plan to shoot out a blazing fire charge, too. Match it up with **polished blackstone pressure plates**.

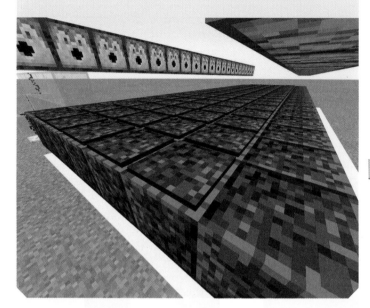

STEP 8

Remember that feeding power to one **dispenser** also powers the **dispenser** immediately to the left and right of it. In Survival, this is especially helpful for saving **redstone** and space. It means all **dispensers** will fire, even with the gaps created in the redstone earlier.

STEP 9

Repeat the process for rigging up the power to every third **dispenser** block, on each side. Ensure the **redstone comparator** is used correctly and test that everything works.

Testing is easier in Creative—but doing so in Survival can be achieved by shooting out something harmless, such as a block.

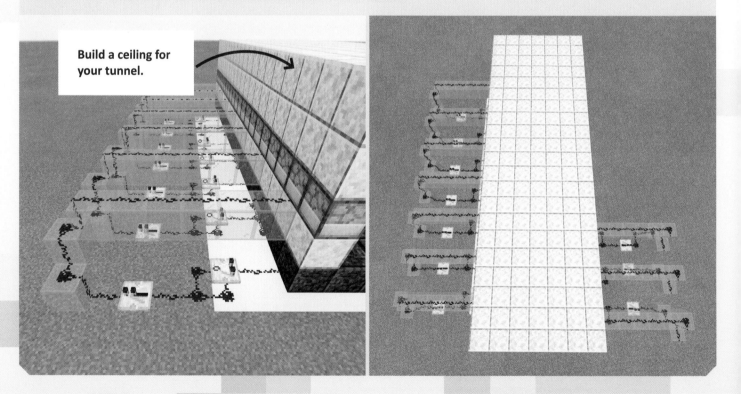

Build a ceiling for your tunnel.

STEP 10

Build the rest of your tunnel and decide what you want to fire from the **dispensers**. If you want to be nice, a helpful item could come out at the halfway stage. This could be a generous thing to do if your gauntlet tunnel is quite long.

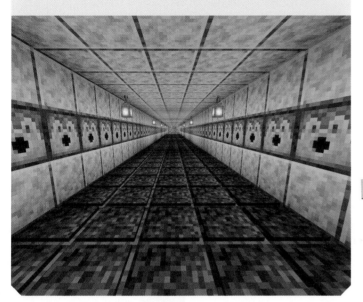

STEP 11

Look at how a build like this, constructed in a large mountain, can appear in a regular Survival game. It may look like an innocent shortcut to a weary wanderer, but you know it isn't!

Perhaps you actually want to mark out the safe route through the gauntlet, using different-colored pressure plates? Another way to highlight the passage to take is to use unusual colored tiles in the ceiling. Good luck building and exploring this vicious valley!

DARK DUNGEON

Create a puzzling world where players need their wits and skills to escape.
Enter these dungeon rooms at your own peril!

MATERIALS

- STONE BLOCKS
- STONE SWITCHES
- IRON DOORS
- REDSTONE DUST
- STICKY PISTON BLOCKS
- LADDERS
- DISPENSER BLOCKS
- GLASS BLOCKS
- LAVA BLOCKS
- SWITCHES
- BUTTONS
- BOW AND ARROWS
- TRAPDOORS
- PRESSURE PLATES

STEP 1

Get ready to experience some escape-style rooms within these baffling builds.
First up is a prison scenario. Make a room that can contain some cells, with a
player beginning in one of the locked locations.

STEP 2

The stone cell has no switches, so that a player can
simply open the door. Sneakily, though, we've placed a
stone switch away from the door, which blends with
the stone wall!

Stone switch

STEP 3

On the other side of the **switch**, **redstone dust** directs its
power to a **sticky piston** under the cell. Place the **sticky
piston** as shown, so that it grabs a block from the cell
floor and pulls it back to reveal a secret exit.

STEP 4

You need a tunnel leading from your secret exit back round to the prison entrance. From here, get ready for the next build.

STEP 5

The next part of the dungeon quest uses a long corridor with a large pitfall. A player will not be able to jump the five-block gap here. Be sure to place a **ladder**, on the side you enter from, to lead a fallen player back up.

STEP 6

At the bottom of the pit are two wooden **pressure plates**. One is positioned in front of a **dispenser** and the other will make a bridge appear to extend over the gap above. Standing on the **pressure plate** powers the bridge for a little over one second, which is not long enough to climb the **ladder** and cross the bridge.

The player must figure out that they should take the dispensed item and drop it on the plate, so that the bridge is powered (extended). They then have enough time to climb and cross the bridge. Pretty smart!

STEP 7

You'll see that when the **dispensed** item is on the plate, the **pistons** push their blocks forward and form a permanent bridge to travel across. Problem solved.

STEP 8

So let's look at making the magical bridge! Run **redstone dust** out of the side of the block that will be powered by the **pressure plate**. This circuit then goes to powering five **sticky pistons**, carefully hidden in the side of the pit wall. Remember that **glass** is a great block to move **redstone** circuits upward.

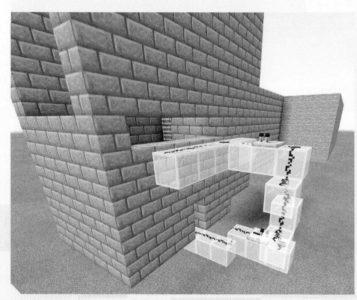

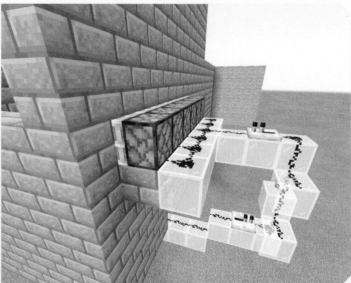

STEP 9

The **sticky pistons** must move out from a single strip of empty blocks in the wall above the pit. Decorate them with stones that cunningly match the rest of the wall.

STEP 10

After the pitfall perils comes a maze challenge. Start by building a platform that extends out to a central maze. Make a maze as simple or complex as you want, using the guide on pages 16-19.

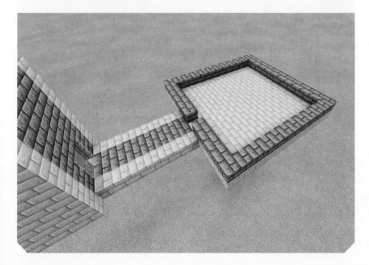

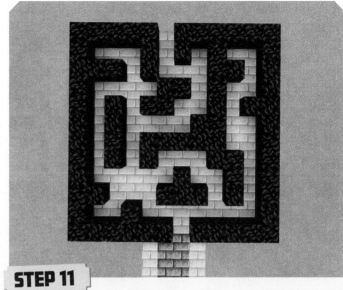

STEP 11

Here, we have installed quite a straightforward maze, but one that will still cause some head scratching.

STEP 12

To be extra mean, this build has a large containing wall around the maze and then a lava floor beneath it. So, players have to solve the maze and can't just walk on through!

At the end of the maze, build another platform to take players to the next dungeon challenge room.

STEP 13

Welcome to the broken hallway challenge, which is simple but frustrating. Build another long corridor, but with a deeper pit below it. Don't forget to add ladders on the starting side, so that fallen players can recover.

STEP 14

You need to add in blocks over the pit, so that a player must navigate a path across. Make the gaps and jumps as difficult as you want, while still being possible to complete. Look at the obstacle course tips on pages 24-29.

STEP 15

After completing the challenge, there's one more dungeon task to face. This time, it's a large room with iron doors on the other side, but no clear switch connected to the door for them to open. Instead, random switches appear all over the room.

STEP 16

Wooden buttons and switches will power a circuit for just over a second. The switch that you select to power the door needs to be far enough away from the exit so that a player must use the bow and arrow to activate it in order to dash through in time.

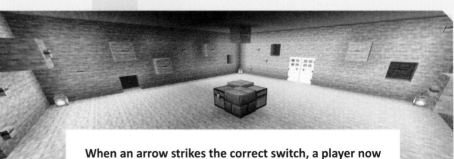

When an arrow strikes the correct switch, a player now has enough time to make their exit. Easy, huh?!

STEP 17

When your **switch** is selected, run a **redstone** circuit from the rear of it, on the outside of the wall, to a block next to the door. Use **trapdoors** to hide this circuit if you like.

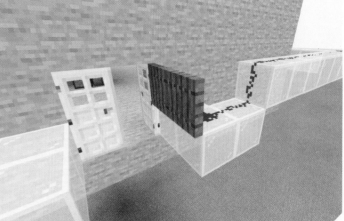

STEP 18

From that exit, you're free to build a final way out of the dungeon. In Survival, for example, it could be fun to build it underground, then have an impressive helix staircase leading back up to the fresh air.

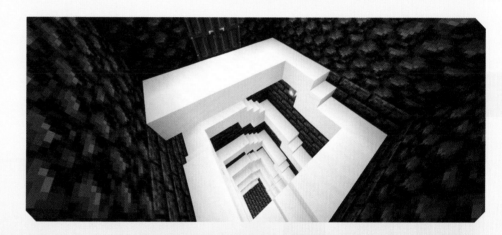

Add as many puzzle elements as you can think of. Be sure to make players think about how to solve the teasers, ramping up the fun and excitement of these mysterious dungeons.

ULTIMATE QUEST

The "ultimate" build in your Minecraft minigames guide! Take a test of puzzle-solving and fighting skills to navigate through these challenging rooms.

MATERIALS

- CONCRETE BLOCKS
- STONE BLOCKS
- TREES AND PLANTS
- DIRT BLOCKS
- CHESTS
- WATER BLOCKS
- WEAPONS
- ARMOR
- WOODEN BUTTONS
- VINES
- IRON DOOR
- PRESSURE PLATES
- REDSTONE DUST
- DISPENSER BLOCKS
- SLABS
- REDSTONE REPEATERS
- BOWS AND ARROWS
- MOB EGGS
- SPAWNER CAGES
- SAND BLOCKS
- CACTI
- PISTONS
- TARGET BLOCKS
- GLASS BLOCKS
- BUTTONS
- STICKY PISTONS
- POTIONS
- ENCHANTED ITEMS
- BEDS
- SOUL SOIL
- WITHER SKULLS
- OBSIDIAN BLOCKS
- CRYING OBSIDIAN BLOCKS
- REDSTONE TORCHES

Based on a classic dungeon crawler theme, we're building ten rooms in total, with eight quest rooms, one secret and one boss fight room. Think about the size, complexity, and theme of your ultimate quest, plus any reward items you'll place or mobs to spawn. We're building in Creative so a range of mobs can appear!

STEP 1

Here is a three-by-three grid of equal-sized rooms. At the moment, there are no ceilings, so you can see the build. To kick off, we have a calm forest and meadow setting.

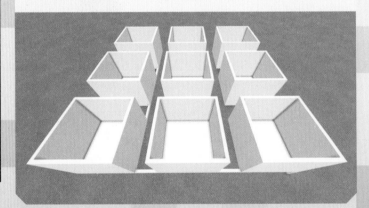

STEP 2

Natural structures such as **trees** and waterfalls suit the style. Paths have been dug, too, and hidden treasure (a **sword, chest plate** and **wooden button** quest item) are stashed in **chests**.

STEP 3

Players must navigate **vines** and tricky blocks—check out the parkour builds on pages 24-29 for ideas. The **wooden button** quest item must be placed by the player next to the **iron door**, so that a player can leave. Add a ceiling and some lighting.

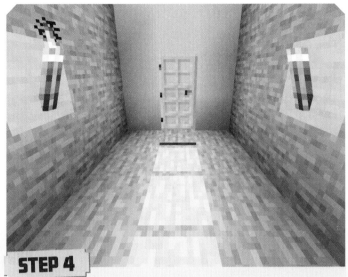

STEP 4

There's an exit corridor from our first room to the next, built in the space between rooms. A **pressure plate** at the end of the corridor activates the next door. The plate also sends power to **redstone dust** placed a block below, so that we can wire events to happen when a player enters.

STEP 5

Run **redstone dust** underneath to a timer, like in the gauntlet and archery games, which is then wired to an upward-facing **dispenser** inside the floor that can be

concealed by a single **slab**. When the **pressure plate** is triggered, the **dispenser** receives pulses and reveals whatever is inside it.

STEP 6

We have used **zombie eggs** in ours. When a player enters and the door slams behind them, a wave of enemies will spawn!

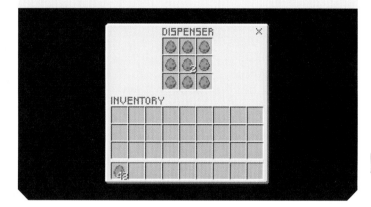

The player must figure out that firing the arrow into the button creates the time needed to be able to leave.

STEP 7

Once the zombies are defeated, the challenge is then to master how to leave the room. Another hidden **chest** has a **bow** and **arrow**, and there's also a **button** that opens the exit—however, it's too far from the **iron door** to allow enough time to get out. The **button** is wired from the outside of the room, and runs to a block next to the **door** to power it.

STEP 8

As an extra "treat", and because it's in Creative, we've placed a **spider spawner** at the top of the tree. We did this with a **spawner cage** and a **spider egg** inside it. Make sure it's not restricted on either side by blocks, and the light level is low enough for it to spawn.

STEP 9

The next two rooms have a desert theme. Varying the theme helps create interest, plus it will make players feel like they are progressing.

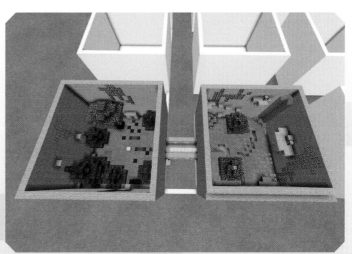

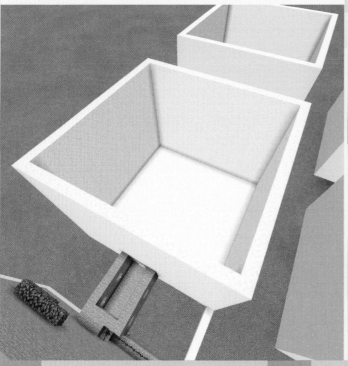

STEP 10

The first of these desert rooms forces a player to navigate technical jumps on a parkour course. The central treasure **chest** has a **button** or quest item, which ultimately allows their release. Perhaps a **helmet** or useable item can also be here, as a reward.

STEP 11

The next room also uses parkour obstacles leading to a **chest**, but it is rigged with yet another **dispenser**, which is concealed under a **slab**. **Endermen** and **husks** are inside to create some chaos!

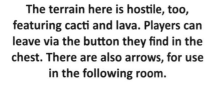

The terrain here is hostile, too, featuring cacti and lava. Players can leave via the button they find in the chest. There are also arrows, for use in the following room.

STEP 12

Here is the first of the cave rooms, boasting a two-stage door-opening process. **Redstone dust** from a floor **pressure plate** leads to a **piston** on the wall. Place a **target block** on the **piston**, so it will rise when the **redstone** is powered by the plate.

STEP 13

Next, run **redstone dust** from the same level as the raised **target block**, toward the exit door. Make sure to build in a delay. When the **target block** is hit with an arrow, it sends a signal to the **door** and opens it.

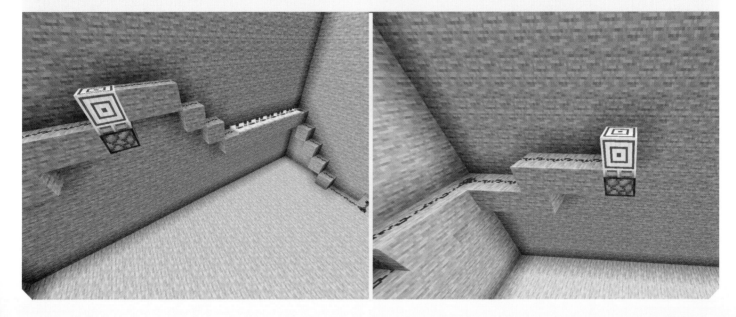

STEP 14

Conceal it as best you can, leaving at least one block between the **redstone dust** and any neighboring blocks. Any placed too close may disrupt the flow.

STEP 15

Players must stand on the **pressure plate**, let the **target block** raise and hit it with enough accuracy to send a pulse to the **door**. The delay helps them get through, but make the timing as tricky as you want.

STEP 16

Make the room look as cave-like as you wish and stash some treasures if you are in a generous mood!

STEP 17

Players should not be too used to only locating **buttons** for the exit... so the second cave room adds a secret exit!

STEP 18

Place two **sticky pistons** next to a two-block high doorway. The **sticky pistons** must be level with the door when powered. Put two blocks that match the surroundings on the **pistons**.

STEP 19

Next, you need a **redstone torch** on a block, facing the side you want to run **redstone dust** toward the secret exit. The **redstone torch** powers the **pistons** by splitting their signal and powering both. The **glass blocks** help show how this might work.

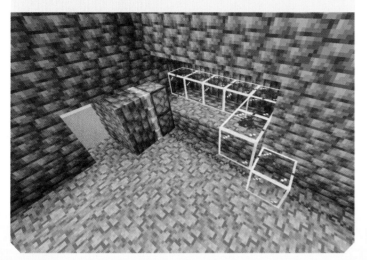

STEP 20

Now, run **redstone dust** from the opposite side of the block that we placed our **redstone torch** on, and attach it to a **button** near the ceiling. Any **repeaters** to lengthen the signal must have their output running toward the **redstone torch**.

STEP 21

When a player activates the **button**, a pulse to the **redstone torch** unpowers it, making the **pistons** retract and exposing the exit. Hide all of the **redstone dust**.

STEP 22

For another monstrous move, there's a **dispenser** above the **button** receiving power. Hidden inside is another **mob egg**. But we have been mega mean and also created an entire ring of **buttons** and **dispensers,** as a cruel challenge to find the exit!

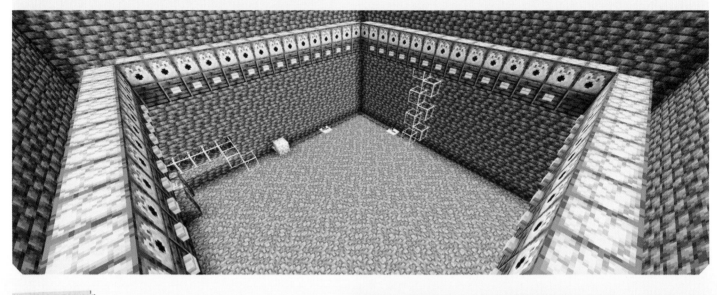

STEP 23

Each **dispenser** has **mob eggs**, items, or both of these. So a player could collect lots of useful things, but also have many enemy fights.

Plus, we've placed one button in one dispenser. It can be used for the regular exit, but a smart player could use it for something else... if they are lucky enough to find it in the first place.

STEP 24

Following the planned route at the start means the player has one last challenging room to conquer before the boss battle. But, there's a secret room in our quest, to surprise anyone smart—or lucky—enough to figure out how to get there.

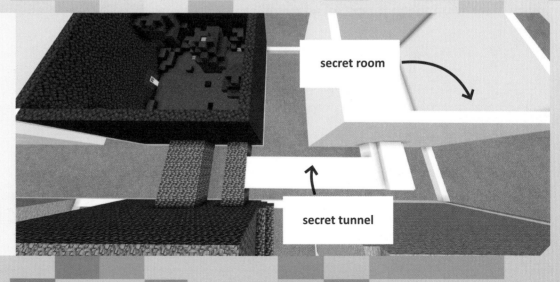

secret room

secret tunnel

STEP 25

If the **button** hidden in the previous room is obtained, it can be used to open another pair of **iron doors** in the hidden exit tunnel. A player can move through the tunnel into the final encounter, or take the secret tunnel to the secret room.

If they used the button to escape the dispenser room, then they won't know this exists. The mysterious tunnel heads to a luxurious secret place, packed with powerful items.

STEP 26

The next room is decked out in Nether-themed blocks. The **pressure plate** powering the entrance door also triggers a **dispenser** that has piglins and piglin brutes. Look out for the **chests** that contain health items and a strong **sword**. Don't miss the final **button** that allows you to exit this terrifying place!

STEP 27

Before the boss room is a calming sanctuary, which creates a false sense of security. The room can have all that's needed to win a big battle, from **weapons** and **potions** to enchanted stuff and health items.

STEP 28

After leaving the prize room, the boss mob is the final encounter. Include a **bed** as a spawn point and a **chest**, in case anything needs to be left behind. It's a very long room with lots of space.

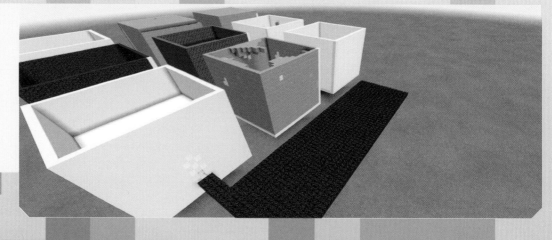

STEP 29

We have opted for a wither boss mob. Usually, it spawns from a t-shape in **soul soil** that has three **wither skulls** along the top. Here, though, the **pressure plates** opening the doors are also connected, via **redstone dust**, to the back of a **dispenser**.

The dispenser is behind a t-shaped soul soil structure that has two skulls already placed. The dispenser has the magic third skull, and when activated, will drop it on the soul soil and cause the wither to spawn. Genius!

STEP 30

As this room is constructed from **obsidian** and crying **obsidian**, the boss is not able to blow it up. The wither is a fierce boss, but defeat it and you will feel like a very worthy winner. It's the ultimate act in your ultimate quest!

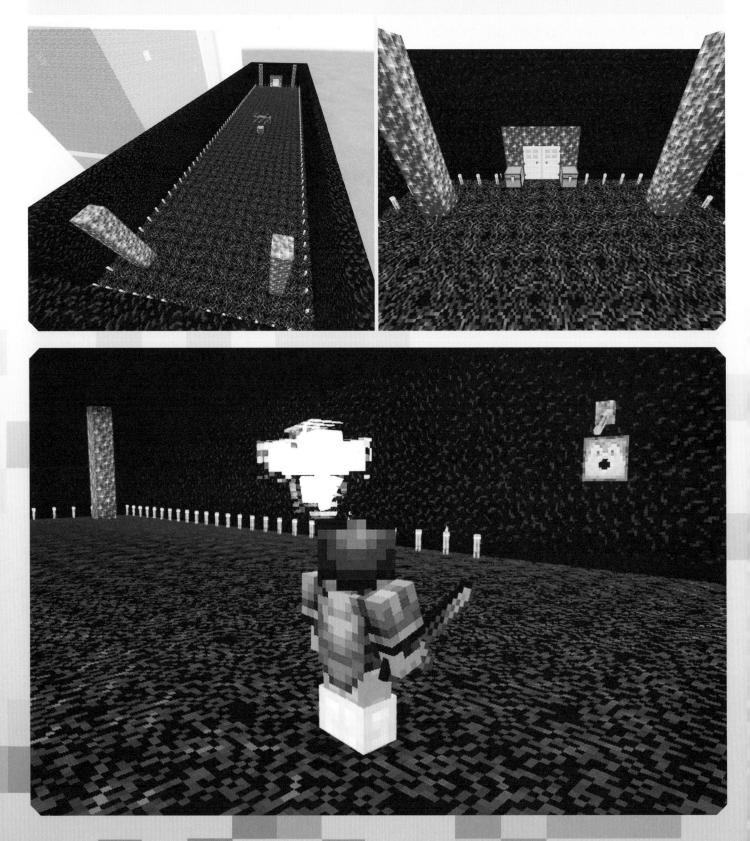